OTHER BOOKS BY WALTER "BIG WALT" ANDERSON

Pledge Brothers
(www.PledgeBrothers.com)

Frat Daze "In The Name of Brotherhood" (video)
(www.Frat-Movie.com)

The Black Greek Book Series
(www.BlackGreekBooks.com)

ABOVE

AND

BEYOND

AN UNAUTHORIZED HISTORY
OF DELTA SIGMA THETA

ABOVE

AND

BEYOND

AN UNAUTHORIZED HISTORY
OF DELTA SIGMA THETA

MH
Milk & Honey
Publishing

http://www.BlackGreekBooks.com

IMPORTANT NOTE: **This book has not been prepared, approved, or licensed by any entity that is associated with Delta Sigma Theta Sorority, Inc.**

Published by:

MH
Milk & Honey Publishing
Arlington, Texas

Library of Congress Catalog Number: 2002110500

ISBN 0-9647596-1-6

More about the author at:

BigWalt.com

And let us not be weary in well doing: for in due season we shall reap; if we faint not.

Galatians 6:9

Δ Σ Θ

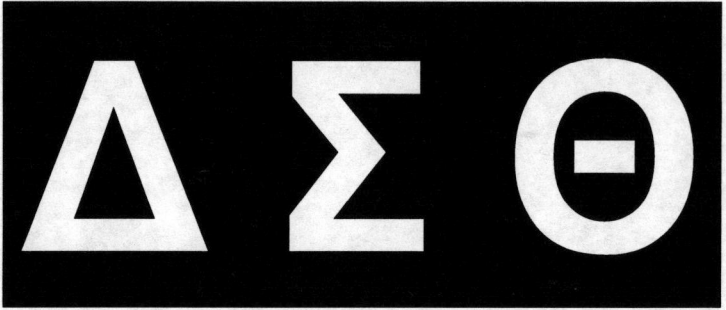

DELTA SIGMA THETA

CONTENTS

Δ Σ Θ

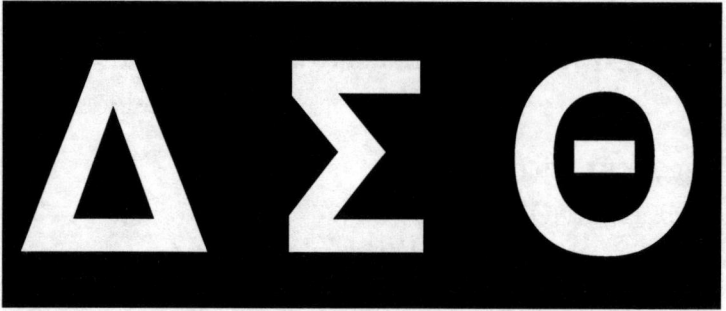

DELTA SIGMA THETA

At Howard University in Washington D. C. twenty-two undergraduate members of Alpha Kappa Alpha Sorority (1908) started a reorganization process that would take their club in a different direction. They came together with their minds, bodies and souls in the Fall Semester of 1912 so that they may accomplish more and do better deeds. Those twenty-two members believed that they could not prosper in the current state of Alpha Kappa Alpha Sorority, although all did not agree on the process for change.

During an era in history where change was rampant there were several reasons for their discontentment and perturbation.

In their eyes, Alpha Kappa Alpha was too closely aligned with the first African American fraternal organization, Alpha Phi Alpha (1906). Also, they wished to be more involved politically as well as communally. Moreover, those twenty-two members wanted to expand their organization and bring the ideas of African American sisterhood nationally.

So with all that in mind, those twenty-two venturous African American women began to restructure Alpha Kappa Alpha.

One of the first acts they would do is seek a name change for their organization, as well as changes for the symbol and colors.

Graduate Alpha Kappa Alpha members became disgruntled to say the least and gave the twenty-two members an enforced deadline to stop such shenanigans. Those twenty-two undergraduate daring members ignored the deadline and continued with their plans, hence an unnatural split of Alpha Kappa Alpha took place.

So on January 13, 1913; those twenty-two courageous, outstanding, exemplary African American young women formally formed their own sorority, the Alpha Chapter of Delta Sigma Theta.

Nellie Quander, a graduate Alpha Kappa Alpha teaching in the Washington DC area, would re-establish Alpha Kappa Alpha since all twenty-two undergraduate active members had abandoned the sorority igniting a feud and rivalry between the two organizations. Over the next few months, Alpha Kappa Alpha and Delta Sigma Theta would spar on a number of legal and administrative levels such as being the first to incorporate its sorority.

Sorority members from each organization would also contend on a shallow level as well, like who could obtain certain male companionships.

But no competition was fiercer than in the classroom! Deltas would try to establish their superiority by maintaining higher grade point averages. In fact, in 1915-16 it was documented that the Deltas had the highest Grade Point Average of all Greek Letter organizations at Howard University and the rest is truly history.

CHAPTER ONE
FOUNDERS

How could anyone begin confabulating about the history of such an illustrious union without speaking about the twenty-two distinguished, esteemed and unforgettable young college women that started it all?

Some of the founders will have more information than others as their lives were better documented making material more readily available such as Bertha Pitts Campbell whom even had a book written about her in 1981 entitled, *Too Young to Be Old: Bertha Pitts Campbell.* But make no mistakes; all twenty-two founders of Delta Sigma Theta had remarkable lives:

Osceola Macarthy Adams, class of 1913, was born on June 13, 1890 in Albany Georgia. During her time at Howard University, she developed a great love for acting and the performing arts.

Founder Osceola Macarthy Adams served as class secretary for Delta Sigma Theta one year and was politically conscious during her years at Howard.

She married the first black dean of the Howard Medical School, Dr. Numa P.G. Adams on September 13, 1913.

Founder Osceola Macarthy Adams graduated from Howard University with a Bachelor of Arts degree and went on to pursue a successful career as an actress utilizing the name of Osceola Archer as a stage designation.

Keeping her ties to Delta Sigma Theta, she served as the National Treasurer of the Sorority from 1921 to 1925.

In 1937 Founder Osceola Macarthy Adams obtained a Masters degree from New York University and went on to fight against racism within the performing arts industry. A hard working drama teacher with natural talents as an actress, she taught and influenced up and coming actors such as Ossie Davis, Sidney Poitier, and Harry Belafonte.

Founder Osceola Macarthy Adams passed away in 1986.

Marguerite **Y**oung **A**lexander, class of 1913, was from Chicago, Illinois. She really embraced the idea of expanding Delta Sigma Theta nationally and was instrumental in doing so. Along with Founder Osceola Macarthy Adams she charted the Lambda Chapter in Chicago.

Many of the other Founders went on to teach after leaving Howard University but Founder Marguerite Young Alexander entered into the business world, which was quite unusual for the era. Most black women were teachers during this time since society was more receptive to this type of profession.

She served as a professional Spanish and French liaison secretary for a Chicago company.

Founder Marguerite Young Alexander remained active with Delta Sigma Theta Incorporated. She assisted in the first housing purchase of the sorority in 1950.

Four short years later she died.

Winona **C**argile **A**lexander was an attractive and sassy young lady from Columbus Georgia. Her father was a minister and she had a birthday only one-day away from her roommate, Founder Bertha Pitts Campbell.

During her time at Howard University, she served as class vice president and was the first custodian of Delta Sigma Theta's Alpha Chapter.

After graduating from Howard, she went on to earn a degree in social work from New York University. She went on to become the first black social worker with the New York City and County Charities.

In 1921 she married an attorney by the name of Edward L. Alexander and they had six children.

Founder Winona Cargile Alexander settled in Jacksonville Florida, while she still maintained her involvement with Delta Sigma Theta. In fact, she attended the 1977 national convention where she spoke on renewing the strength of Delta Sigma Theta, and was present at the 1981 national conference.

She lived 9 scores plus before passing away on October 16, 1984.

Ethel **C**uff **B**lack, class of 1915, was the only Founder that had not graduated after the spring semester of 1914 due to sickness.

Founder Ethel Cuff Black was from Wilmington, Delaware; she came from a family of means. Very intellectual in her own right, Founder Ethel Cuff Black graduated with the highest scholastic average at her high school.

While attending Howard University, she was in the choir, and participated in other campus activities such as the newly formed YWCA where she was the collegiate chairperson from 1911-1912.

She married David Horton Black and was the first Black teacher in Richmond County, New York.

Founder Ethel Cuff Black continued to obey the call of Delta Sigma Theta. She charted the Queens Alumnae Chapter and was present at many conventions, banquets and functions of Delta Sigma Theta in the latter years of her life.

Founder Ethel Cuff Black retired from the New York City school system where she taught Social Studies for a great number of years.

Bertha Pitts Campbell, truly an extraordinary woman. One could very well argue the fact that out of all the founders her life has been documented the most. Born in 1889, in Winfield Kansas to Hubbard and Ida Sydney Pitts she was an exceptional educational talent. After the Pitt's family moved to Colorado, Bertha's grandmother, Eliza Butler, fostered and groomed her educationally. Founder Bertha Pitts Campbell would be the only African American to enroll at her high school in 1903. This would only be the first of many great accomplishments in her life. She went on to graduate from the all white high school in 1908 as valedictorian, even an incredible accomplishment today so just imagine how educationally and mentally strong this young lady was to achieve such honor in 1908!

ABOVE

AND

BEYOND

AN UNAUTHORIZED HISTORY
OF DELTA SIGMA THETA

During that same year Founder Bertha
Pitts Campbell graduated summa cum laude
from high school, Alpha Kappa Alpha Sorority
was formed at Howard University.
After declining a scholarship offer to
attend an all white College in Colorado she
decided on attending Howard University in the
nations capital of Washington D.C.
Howard University was a progressive
black university with a beautiful campus. It was
too expensive for Founder Bertha Pitts
Campbell's family to afford but with her
promising future she received financial
assistance to attend in 1909.
While at Howard Founder Bertha Pitts
Campbell would align herself with twenty-one
other outstanding young women and they would
become members of the social sorority Alpha
Kappa Alpha.
Founder Bertha Pitts Campbell rose to the
top of the Alpha Kappa Alpha ranks quickly as
well as others from the twenty-two. And after the
"old" Alpha Kappa Alpha members graduated
the young twenty-two began entertaining ideas
for reorganizing the sorority. Founder Bertha
Pitts Campbell was passionate about

nationalizing the sorority. Also, she believed
that the sorority should serve the community and
have a political presence.

Founder Bertha Pitts Campbell attended
the Teachers College and so did many of the
other twenty-two.

After graduating from Howard she
married Earl Campbell and had a son. A tragic
accident took the life of her son and just three
short years later her husband died of a sudden
heart attack.

She was a teacher and tireless worker for
racial equality in Seattle Washington. She was a
ranking active member of the YWCA and later
received an achievement award from that
association.

She remained loyal to Delta Sigma Theta
through out her life. At the age of 92 she led
10,000 members of Delta Sigma Theta on a
commemorative March of the 1913 suffrage
march, which was the first public act of Delta
Sigma Theta as a sorority!

Founder Bertha Pitts Campbell had a book
written about her in 1981 entitled, *Too Young to
Be Old: Bertha Pitts Campbell.* The book is a
rare find and a definite keepsake.

Only a chosen few in this world will have
an opportunity to witness, and accomplish all
that she did in her life. Founder Bertha Pitts

Campbell passed away in 1990; she was 100 years old!

Zephyr **C**hisom **C**arter, class of 1913, was born on November 14, 1891 in El Paso, Texas.

She was high spirited and very popular at Howard University where she participated in numerous campus activities, such as the Literary and Social Club and student chapter of the NAACP. Also, Founder Zephyr Chisom Carter served as office of reporter.

After Howard she moved backed to Texas where she taught in San Antonio before moving on to California to sing background for motion pictures and television shows; singing was her first love.

Founder Zephyr Chisom Carter attended national functions of Delta Sigma Theta Inc., before passing away in 1976. She did marry and had children.

Edna Brown Coleman was from Washington, DC. Her father was a former slave. She graduated valedictorian of her high school before moving on to Howard where she was considered to be the brightest girl in the graduating class of 1913.

During her time at Howard University, she served as class President.

An advocate of reorganizing Alpha Kappa Alpha, considered instrumental in the many meetings held to reorganize the sorority, she felt that the sorority was too pretentious in its current state.

Founder Edna Brown Coleman married one of the founding fathers of Omega Psi Phi (1911), Frank Coleman.

Jessie McGuire Dent, class of 1913, was born in Galveston, Texas in 1891.

Founder Jessie McGuire Dent was Delta Sigma Theta's first recording secretary.

Her achievements were great when she left Howard as she sued the Galveston Independent School District for equal salaries for blacks and won!

Her portrait is in the Texas Culture Archives.

Founder Jessie McGuire Dent continued to fight for her community and until her death.

Frederica **C**hase **D**odd, class of 1914, was born in Dallas, Texas to attorney Frederic and Fannie Chase. Her father was one of the early black lawyers in the state of Texas.

Founder Frederica Chase Dodd was known for her beauty and eloquent style.

At Howard, she served as president of the YWCA and after Howard she organized the first black women YWCA in Dallas.

Founder Frederica Chase Dodd was the first sergeant at arms for Delta Sigma Theta and she remained active with the sorority well after she graduated from Howard University, establishing the Eta Beta Chapter of Delta Sigma Theta in Dallas, Texas.

She married John H. Dodd, a Howard Medical School graduate.

Founder Frederica Chase Dodd died on January 21, 1972.

Myra Davis Hemmings, class of 1913, was born in Gonzalez, Texas in 1887. During her time at Howard University, she developed tremendous leadership capabilities.

Founder Myra Davis Hemmings served as Delta Sigma Theta's first president; she was also the president before reorganization.

After leaving Howard she married John "Pop" Hemmings.

Founder Myra Davis Hemmings remained active with Delta Sigma Theta throughout her life. She served the Grand Office as vice president, she was director of the Southwest Region and she helped charter the Alumnae Chapter in San Antonio where she taught 50 years as an English teacher.

Founder Myra Davis Hemmings rich and full life came to an end in 1958. She was highly regarded as a natural born leader.

Olive C Jones, class of 1913, was considered the most musically inclined of the twenty-two Founders. She loved playing the piano and had an undying love for music.

She was a music instructor in her hometown of Washington, DC after she graduated from Howard.

Founder Olive C Jones was one of two Founders that never married. In the latter years of her life she lost touch with Delta Sigma Theta.

Jimmie Bugg Middleton, class of 1913, was from Lynchburg, VA. She was the first to be born of the twenty-two Founders.

She enrolled in the Teachers College at Howard.

After graduation she married Dr. Charles Clayton Middleton and they had two daughters.

When Founder Jimmie Bugg Middleton received her Masters degree from Howard University in 1936, her youngest daughter received her Bachelors.

Founder Jimmie Bugg Middleton spent years trying to establish a chapter of Delta Sigma Theta in NC and in 1938 she finally saw the creation of the Alpha Zeta Sigma Chapter in Raleigh, NC.

She was the Dean of a North Carolina High School and was the national Treasurer of the National Association of College Women.

Founder Jimmie Bugg Middleton died on February 17, 1967.

Pauline **O**berdorfer **M**inor, class of
1914, was born in Charlottesville, VA but was
raised by her aunt and uncle in Philadelphia, PA.
She graduated valedictorian of the
Teachers College at Howard in 1914.
She was the Alpha Chapter's first
Treasurer and she was the president of the
Teacher's College.
After Howard, Founder Oberdorfer Minor
became a soprano soloist and hymn writer (wrote
a book of hymns entitled *Get Off the Judgment
Seat*) and taught school in Alabama, South
Carolina and Pennsylvania.
Founder Oberdorfer Minor lost contact
with Delta Sigma Theta in her later years.
She died on January 23, 1963.

Vashti Turley Murphy, class of 1914, was from Washington, DC.

She served as class vice-president at Howard and was a member of the student NAACP.

Founder Vashti Turley Murphy was sometimes referred to as "Ms. Vash". She had five daughters; all became Deltas!

She married Carl Murphy, a publisher of an African American newspaper in Baltimore.

Founder Vashti Turley Murphy chartered the Epsilon Sigma Chapter of Delta Sigma Theta in Baltimore, Maryland. She continued to be involved with Delta Sigma Theta until her death.

Naomi Sewell Richardson, class of 1914, was from Washingtonville, NY.

At Howard she supported the reorganization of Alpha Kappa Alpha.

After graduation she taught in the East Saint Louis School system where racism was rampant before moving on to teach in the New York City School System.

She married Charles Richardson and remained active in the community. Founder Sewell Richardson was honored by the Mid-Hudson Chapter of Delta Sigma Theta on her 90th birthday.

She was the last surviving Founder. She died in 1993 in her hometown.

Mamie Reddy Rose, class of 1913, was the first Founder to die; February 17, 1919, only six years after Delta Sigma Theta was created.

During her time at Howard University, she served as the President of the Literary and Social Club and received many awards for her dramatic readings.

She married a reverend, James E. Rose, and became a homemaker.

Eliza P Shippen, class of 1912, was from Washington, DC where she graduated number one from her high school. She followed her father's footsteps and decided to attend Howard University.

She was a member of the Teachers Club and graduated magna cum laude from the Teachers College at Howard.

Founder Eliza P Shippen went on to receive her Masters Degree from Columbia University and she was the only one of the Founders to obtain a PHD. When she received her PHD in English from the University of Pennsylvania in 1944, Founder Eliza P Shippen had distinguished herself by being one of a small percentage of African American women in the country to have received a PHD.

She never married and remained active with the sorority and community until her death in 1981.

Florence Letcher Toms, class of 1913, was from Washington, DC. She was the tallest of the twenty-two and was called "Flossie".

She married Charles Toms, and became an assistant principal at Garnett-Patterson Junior High School in Washington, DC.

She obtained a Masters Degree from New York University while remaining active in many civic organizations.

Founder Letcher Toms was an avid collector of elephants (see chapter on Delta Knowledge).

Ethel Carr Watson, class of 1913, was from Parkersburg, West Virginia.

During her time at Howard University, she was an active member of the Literary and Social Club where she served as Treasurer.

After Howard she enjoyed a long, 30 years, fulfilling career as a Teacher.

After teaching she embarked on a career as a dramatic performer, acting in theaters.

Wertie Blackwell Weaver, class of 1913, hometown was Kansas City, MO.

After leaving Howard where she was a strong supporter of the Alpha Chapter of Delta Sigma Theta, she taught in the Public School System of her home state.

Later she became an author and expressed her feelings in a novel about poor blacks and the south. The book was called *Valley of the Poor*.

She joined the Nu Sigma Chapter of Delta Sigma Theta as she continued her involvement with the sorority.

Madree Penn White, class of 1914, graduated with honors from her high school in Omaha, Nebraska.

She passed on offers to attend other schools before deciding on Howard.

During her time at Howard University, she participated in numerous campus activities. She was the first female editor of the school newspaper; she was the vice president of the student chapter of the NAACP, and much more.

Founder Madree Penn White was the driving force behind the establishment of Delta Sigma Theta. She was the first to entertain the idea and to share her thoughts with others. She even convinced other sorority members that were not quite sure that reorganization was the way to go. Her influence was tremendous!

Founder Madree Peen White developed the new sorority's constitution, by-laws, rituals, and laid the tracks in order for other chapters to be established. She was the second president of the Alpha Chapter.

After graduation she even served as the National Journalist of Delta Sigma Theta for a short time. She chartered the Lambda Sigma Chapter and remained active with Delta Sigma Theta until her passing.

Edith Motte Young, class of 1913, was from North Carolina.

She was Delta Sigma Theta's first secretary. She was a close friend of Edgar Love, one of the founding fathers of Omega Psi Phi, while she attended Howard.

After Howard, she taught at Claflin College in South Carolina before moving on and receiving her Masters Degree from Oberlin College.

Founder Edith Motte Young was present at the 40th anniversary of Delta Sigma Theta in 1953.

Those are the twenty-two. Quite a group of superb, outstanding young women, all of whom were top students amongst their high school and college peers.

All twenty-two Founders graduated from Howard University. Some went on to achieve Master Degrees with one even obtaining a PHD!

So what does this say? It only says one thing; the twenty-two Founders of Delta Sigma Theta had it going on! They set a precedence of excellence! Quite simply they were the best, on top of their game, and to think that they were motivated to serve others make them truly remarkable and unforgettable.

THE GREEK ALPHABET

A	alpha
B	beta
Γ	gamma
Δ	delta
E	epsilon
Z	zêta
H	êta
Θ	thêta
I	Iota
K	kappa
Λ	lambda
M	mu
N	nu
Ξ	xi
O	omicron
Π	pi
P	rho
Σ	sigma
T	tau
Y	upsilon
Φ	phi
X	chi
Ψ	psi
Ω	omega

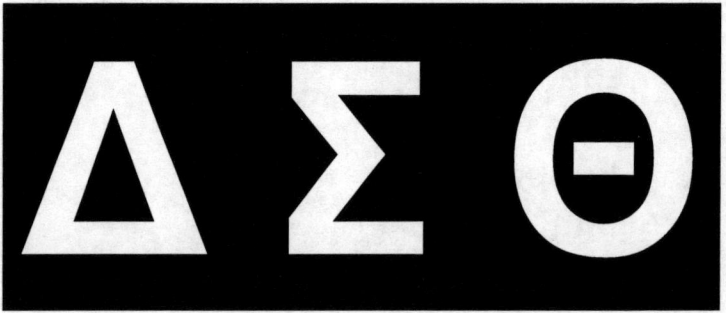

DELTA SIGMA THETA

CHAPTER TWO
DELTA KNOWLEDGE
! FOR YOUR EYES-ONLY !

Delta Sigma Theta Vital Information

<u>World Wide Headquarters</u>:
Delta Sigma Theta Sorority, Inc.
1707 New Hampshire Avenue, NW
Washington, DC 20009

Phone number: (202) 986-2400
Web address: www.deltasigmatheta.org

Date Founded:	January 13, 1913

Location Founded:	Howard University

Official Flower: African Violet

The violet symbolizes modesty and represents the relationship established with the brothers of Omega Psi Phi.

What are the ties to Omega Psi Phi anyway? *The relationship with Omega Psi Phi goes back to the very beginning of Delta Sigma Theta. It could very well be argued that Omega Psi Phi "influenced" the reorganization of Alpha Kappa Alpha by challenging young members of the sorority to create an organization that had a wider scope and vision than what it presently had. Frank Coleman one of the founders of Omega Psi Phi married one of the founders of Delta Sigma, Edna Brown, soon after graduation. The two had been engaged while attending Howard University.*

In 1913, Grace Coleman, the sister of Frank Coleman was initiated into Delta Sigma Theta. She became the Chapter's President in 1914 solidifying the relationship with Omega Psi Phi, hence the phrases "Coleman Love" or "The Coleman Family" as many Deltas today (almost 100 years later) consider the men of Omega Psi Phi as their brothers. Note: *There is no legal constitutional bond or establishment between Delta Sigma Theta and Omega Psi Phi.*

Official Symbol: Fortitude

The Fortitude symbol is meant to inspire women to move persistently forward to meet the challenges of life. She represents love, courage, hope, and determination.

The extended hands represent the giving of one self to others. The statue is shown pushing forward, the tension on her thigh is indicative of her strength.

A replica of the Fortitude sculpture can be seen on Howard University's campus, it was erected in 1976.

Traditional Symbol: Elephant

What is the meaning of the Elephant? What does the elephant represent? These questions have been posed quite often and some even consider them mysteries, however there are no mystical underlying forces behind the elephant.

Simply, one of the Founders of Delta Sigma Theta, Florence Letcher Toms, enjoyed collecting elephants and upon her death her collection (which was considerable) was donated to Delta Sigma Theta. Out of remembrance, Deltas began collecting elephants, as it was even an initiative of the organization.

From there the tradition grew to individual members of Delta Sigma Theta collecting elephants with the first twenty-two being that of elephants that have their trunks up.

The trunk up represents the establishment of high goals, as the elephant is a good luck symbol to the Deltas within itself, a lucky charm with history behind it.

Official Colors: Crimson and Cream

Crimson (red) represents courage and Cream (white) represents purity.

Sorority Call: high pitch "OO-OOP!"

Motto: "Intelligence is the Torch of Wisdom"

The 22 Founders (in alphabetical order):

Δ Osceola Macarthy Adams

Δ Marguerite Young Alexander

△ Winona Cargile Alexander

△ Ethel Cuff Black

△ Bertha Pitts Campbell

△ Zephyr Chisom Carter

△ Edna Brown Coleman

△ Jessie McGuire Dent

△ Frederica Chase Dodd

△ Myra Davis Hemmings

△ Olive C. Jones

△ Jimmie Bugg Middleton

△ Pauline Oberdorfer Minor

△ Vashti Turley Murphy

△ Naomi Sewell Richardson

△ Mamie Reddy Rose

△ Eliza P. Shippen

Δ Florence Letcher Toms

Δ Ethel Carr Watson

Δ Wertie Blackwell Weaver

Δ Madree Penn White

Δ Edith Motte Young

THE DELTA OATH

I will strive to reach the highest educational, moral, and spiritual efficiency which I can possibly attain.

I will never lower my aims for any temporary benefit which might be gained.

I will endeavor to preserve my health, for however great one's mental and moral strength may be, physical weakness prevents the accomplishment of much that otherwise might be done.

I will close my ears and seal my lips to slanderous gossip.

I will labor to ennoble the ideals and purify the atmosphere of the home.

I will always protest against the double standard of morals.

I will take an active interest in the welfare of my country, using my influence toward enactment of laws for the protection of the unfortunate and weak, and for the repeal of those depriving human beings of their privileges and rights.
I will never belittle my race, but encourage all to hold it in honor and esteem.

I will not shrink from undertaking what seems wise and good because I labor under the double handicap of race and sex but, striving to preserve a calm mind with a courageous spirit, barring bitterness from my heart, I will strive all the more earnestly to reach the goal.

by Mary Church Terrell (1914)

TEST YOUR DELTA IQ

PART ONE

Think you know all there is to know about the beginnings of Delta Sigma Theta? Sure, some answers come right out of this book, so if you were reading closely, you should do fine. And that doesn't mean you should peak back to the chapter for the answers – see what you can remember on your own! When you're done with the quiz, be sure to turn to the back of the book and write in your score.
Good Luck!

1) Where was Delta Sigma Theta Founded?
   a. Hampton University
   b. George Washington University
   c. Howard University
   d. Tuskegee University

2) Who was the only person to be President of Alpha Kappa Alpha and Delta Sigma Theta?
   a. Myra Hemmings
   b. Madree White
   c. Osceola Macarthy Adams
   d. Bertha Pitts Campbell

3) How many Founders of Delta Sigma Theta?
   a. 12
   b. 22
   c. 32
   d. 19

4) What Greek Letters mean Delta Sigma Theta?
   a. ΛΣΘ
   b. ΔΣΘ
   c. ΣΘΔ
   d. ΔΣΦ

5) How long did it take for Delta Sigma Theta Sorority to perform its first public act?
   a. 1month
   b. 2months
   c. 6months
   d. 1year

THE DELTA HYMN

by   Alice Dunbar
         Florence Cole Talbert

Delta! With glowing hearts we praise thee
For the strength thy love bestows
For the glowing grace of thy sisterhood
And the pow'r that from it flows
Keep in us a strong endeavor
And our souls to rapture raise.
Delta lights the flame and ever
Warms our hearts her bond to praise
Delta Sigma Theta! We rejoice in thee!
Delta Sigma Theta! We pledge thee loyalty.
Devoted to truth
A bond of our youth
That keeps our hearts clean and pure to the end
The bright gleam of thy vision has lighted the
world
Delta Sigma Theta!
Our Own!

ABOVE
AND
BEYOND

AN UNAUTHORIZED HISTORY
OF DELTA SIGMA THETA

CHAPTER THREE
HOLDING DOWN A DREAM

In March of 1913 Delta Sigma Theta Sorority participated in the suffrage parade that sought a woman's right to vote. Against many obstacles the sorority marched down the streets of Washington, DC amid chaos and animosity.

The Alpha Chapter had an important mission to fulfill after the creation of its sorority, political and social advocating would be a top priority as well as the establishment of chapters outside of Howard University.

BETA TO OMEGA CHAPTERS
A LOOK AT THE SINGLE GREEK WORD CHAPTERS

Beta Chapter   February 5, 1914

The establishment of the Beta Chapter at Wilberforce University in Ohio was very significant, it was the second chapter of Delta Sigma Theta and it was seen as an equal in the bond of sisterhood. This was necessary in order for the sorority to move forward and nationalize.

The Beta Chapter could make decisions and set guidelines on their own in which they did. In fact, it has been said that the Beta Chapter raised the bar even higher than what the Alpha Chapter originally required.

Beta Chapter Founders:
Freddie Billings
Nakomis Boyd
Helen Ferguson
Margaret Glass
Ruby Martin
Beatrice Mason
Marie Ody
Bernice Sandler
Annie Singleton
Iolyn Springfield

Gamma Chapter
University of Pennsylvania 1918

Delta Chapter
Iowa 1919

Epsilon Chapter
Ohio State University 1919

Zeta Chapter
University of Cincinnati 1920

Eta Chapter
Fort Valley 1944

Theta Chapter
Duquesne 1946

Iota Chapter
Boston 1922

Kappa Chapter
University of California Berkeley 1921

Lambda Chapter
University of Chicago 1947

Mu Chapter
University of Pittsburgh 1921

Nu Chapter
Michigan 1921

Xi Chapter
Louisville 1922

Omicron Chapter
Nebraska 1922

Pi Chapter
University of California (UCLA) 1923

Rho Chapter
Columbia University 1924

Sigma Chapter
Clark Atlanta University 1924

Tau Chapter
Wayne State University 1924

Upsilon Chapter
University of Southern California (USC) 1924

Phi Chapter
Drake 1925

Chi Chapter
Indianapolis 1925

Psi Chapter
University of Kansas 1925

Omega Chapter
Cleveland 1925

You can notice how most of the <u>single Greek word</u> chapters were established during the early years of Delta Sigma Theta and shows the progression of the sorority.

In 1915, 1916 and 1917 the nation was involved in World War I and as you see from above no chapters were established during this time.

Since 1913 Delta Sigma Theta has grown to a membership of over 250,000 with 950 chapters worldwide.

A comprehensive list of Chapters of Delta Sigma Theta is below:

A

1913 [Alpha] Howard
1925 [Alpha Alpha] Kansas City (KS)
1925 [Alpha Beta] Fisk
1926 [Alpha Gamma] Morgan State University
1926 [Alpha Delta] West Virginia State
1927 [Alpha Epsilon]
1927 [Alpha Zeta] Talladega
1929 [Alpha Eta] Virginia State
1930 [Alpha Theta] Lincoln University (MO)
1930 [Alpha Iota] Wiley
1930 [Alpha Kappa] Houston-Tillotson

1931 [Alpha Lambda] North Carolina Central
1932 [Alpha Mu] North Carolina A & T State
1932 [Alpha Nu] U of IL at Champaign-Urbana
1934 [Alpha Xi] South Carolina State University
1934 [Alpha Omicron] U of WA - Seattle
1934 [Alpha Pi] Kentucky State
1934 [Alpha Rho] Shaw University
1934 [Alpha Sigma]
1934 [Alpha Tau] Southern
1934 [Alpha Upsilon] LeMoyne-Owen
1934 [Alpha Phi] Wichita
1934 [Alpha Chi] Tennessee State
1934 [Alpha Psi]
1936 [Alpha Omega] St. Louis, MO City-Wide

B

1914 [Beta] Wilberforce
1937 [Beta Alpha] Florida A & M
1937 [Beta Beta]
1937 [Beta Gamma] Dillard
1937 [Beta Delta] Dallas
1937 [Beta Epsilon] Virginia Union
1937 [Beta Zeta] Kansas State Teachers
1937 [Beta Eta] Alabama State
1937 [Beta Theta] Phoenix
1937 [Beta Iota] D. C. Teachers
1937 [Beta Kappa] Livingstone
1938 [Beta Lambda] University of Toledo

1938 [Beta Mu] San Diego State
1938 [Beta Nu] Gary
1938 [Beta Xi]
1938 [Beta Omicron] Corpus Christi
1938 [Beta Pi] Bluefield
1938 [Beta Rho] Fort Worth
1938 [Beta Sigma]
1938 [Beta Tau] Milwaukee
1939 [Beta Upsilon] Langston
1939 [Beta Phi]
1939 [Beta Chi] Lane
1940 [Beta Psi] Portland, OR City-Wide
1940 [Beta Omega]

Γ 1918 [Gamma]University of Pennslyvania
1940 [Gamma Alpha] Xavier University of LA
1941 [Gamma Beta] Washburn
1941 [Gamma Gamma] Philander Smith
1941 [Gamma Delta] Galveston
1942 [Gamma Epsilon] Texas College
1942 [Gamma Zeta] Morris Brown College
1942 [Gamma Eta] East St. Louis IL
1943 [Gamma Theta] Dayton
1943 [Gamma Iota] Hampton University
1943 [Gamma Kappa] Buffalo, NY City-Wide
1945 [Gamma Lambda] Johnson C. Smith
1947 [Gamma Mu] Knoxville
1947 [Gamma Nu] Indiana University

1947 [Gamma Xi] Omaha, NE City-Wide
1948 [Gamma Omicron] Evanston
1948 [Gamma Pi] Allen
1948 [Gamma Rho] St. Augustine's
1948 [Gamma Sigma]
1948 [Gamma Tau] Tuskegee
1948 [Gamma Upsilon] Benedict
1948 [Gamma Phi] Winston-Salem State
1948 [Gamma Chi] Claflin
1948 [Gamma Psi] Tougaloo Southern Christian
1948 [Gamma Omega] Meharry Medical

Δ   1919 [Delta] Iowa
1949 [Delta Alpha] Bethune-Cookman
1949 [Delta Beta] Eastern Michigan University
1949 [Delta Gamma] Texas Southern
1949 [Delta Delta] Alabama A & M
1949 [Delta Epsilon] Alcorn State
1950 [Delta Zeta] Montclair, NJ City-Wide
1950 [Delta Eta] Uni. of Arkansas at Pine Bluff
1950 [Delta Theta] Cal State - Sacramento
1950 [Delta Iota] Grambling State
1951 [Delta Kappa] Central State
1951 [Delta Lambda] Youngstown
1952 [Delta Mu] Maryland State
1952 [Delta Nu] Savannah State University
1952 [Delta Xi] Fayetteville State University

1952 [Delta Omicron] St. Paul's
1952 [Delta Pi] Jackson State
1952 [Delta Rho] Albany State
1952 [Delta Sigma]
1953 [Delta Tau] Cheyney State
1953 [Delta Upsilon] Western Michigan
1953 [Delta Phi] Ball State
1953 [Delta Chi] Elizabeth City State
1954 [Delta Psi] Detroit City-Wide
1955 [Delta Omega] Bishop

E 1919 [Epsilon] Ohio State
1958 [Epsilon Alpha] Delaware State
1960 [Epsilon Beta] University of Texas at Austin
1960 [Epsilon Gamma] Pennsylvania State
1960 [Epsilon Delta] Temple University
1960 [Epsilon Epsilon] Michigan State
1962 [Epsilon Zeta] California State-Los Angeles
1962 [Epsilon Eta] Stillman
1962 [Epsilon Theta] Norfolk State
1963 [Epsilon Iota] Ohio
1963 [Epsilon Kappa] University of Memphis
[Epsilon Lambda]
1964 [Epsilon Mu] Kent State
[Epsilon Nu] San Francisco, CA City-Wide
[Epsilon Xi] Southern Illinois Uni.-Edwardsville
1965 [Epsilon Omicron] Bowling Green State

1965 [Epsilon Pi] Long Island, NY City-Wide
1965 [Epsilon Rho] University of Dayton
1965 [Epsilon Sigma]
1966 [Epsilon Tau] New York, NY City-Wide
1966 [Epsilon Upsilon] Hartford, CT City-Wide
1966 [Epsilon Phi] Philadelphia, PA City-Wide
1966 [Epsilon Chi] Southern Uni.-New Orleans
1966 [Epsilon Psi] Uni. of Missouri-Columbia
1966 [Epsilon Omega] Barber-Scotia

Z

1920 [Zeta]University of Cincinnati
1967 [Zeta Alpha] Akron, OH City-Wide
1967 [Zeta Beta] Wichita State
1968 [Zeta Gamma] Youngstown State
1968 [Zeta Delta] Bowie State
1968 [Zeta Epsilon] Coppin
1968 [Zeta Zeta] Truman State University
1968 [Zeta Eta] University of North Texas
1968 [Zeta Theta] Purdue
1968 [Zeta Iota] Northern Illinois
1969 [Zeta Kappa] Northern Michigan
1969 [Zeta Lambda] Central Missouri State
1969 [Zeta Mu] Miami (OH)
1969 [Zeta Nu] Indiana State
1969 [Zeta Xi] Madison, WI City-Wide
1969 [Zeta Omicron] Greensboro
1969 [Zeta Pi] Denver, CO City-Wide

1969 [Zeta Rho] Ferris State University
1969 [Zeta Sigma] University of Houston
1969 [Zeta Tau] Florida Memorial
1969 [Zeta Upsilon] San Antonio, TX City-Wide
1969 [Zeta Phi] Georgia State
1969 [Zeta Chi] Southern Illinois University
1969 [Zeta Psi] Georgia
1969 [Zeta Omega] Lincoln University PA

H 1944 [Eta] Fort Valley
1969 [Eta Alpha] Mississippi Valley State
1969 [Eta Beta] Prairie View A&M
1970 [Eta Gamma] Kansas State
1970 [Eta Delta] Texas Woman' s
1970 [Eta Epsilon] West Texas State A&M
1970 [Eta Zeta] Western Kentucky
1970 [Eta Eta] Western Illinois
1970 [Eta Theta] Paine
1970 [Eta Iota] New Mexico
1970 [Eta Kappa] Spelman
1970 [Eta Lambda] Texas Tech
1970 [Eta Mu]
1970 [Eta Nu] Miles
1970 [Eta Xi] University of Tennessee - Martin
1970 [Eta Omicron] Morehead State
1970 [Eta Pi] Missouri - St. Louis
1970 [Eta Rho] Eastern Kentucky

1970 [Eta Sigma] Tulsa
1970 [Eta Tau] Virginia Commonwealth
1970 [Eta Upsilon] Murray State
1970 [Eta Phi] Voorhees
1970 [Eta Chi] University of Nevada-Las Vegas
1970 [Eta Psi] Lamar
1970 [Eta Omega] San Jose State

Θ   1946 [Theta] Duquesne
1971 [Theta Alpha] Northwestern
1971 [Theta Beta] Indiana, PA City-Wide
1971 [Theta Gamma] Stephen F. Austin State
1971 [Theta Delta] Illinois State University
1971 [Theta Epsilon] Bradley
1971 [Theta Zeta] Eastern Illinois
1971 [Theta Eta] Cleveland, OH City-Wide
1971 [Theta Theta] Central Michigan
1971 [Theta Iota] North Carolina-Wilmington
1971 [Theta Kappa] Jarvis Christian
1971 [Theta Lambda] Kansas State - Emporia
1971 [Theta Mu] Oklahoma State
1971 [Theta Nu] Texas A/M Uni. - Commerce
1971 [Theta Xi] Southwestern Louisiana
1971 [Theta Omicron] Culver-Stockton
1971 [Theta Pi] Rust
1971 [Theta Rho] Tennessee-Chattanooga
1971 [Theta Sigma] Georgia Southwestern
1971 [Theta Tau] Valdosta State

1971 [Theta Upsilon] William Paterson University
1971 [Theta Phi] Columbus State
1971 [Theta Chi] Glassboro, NJ City-Wide
1971 [Theta Psi] Los Angeles, CA City-Wide
1971 [Theta Omega] Marshall

I

1922 [Iota] Boston
1971 [Iota Alpha] James Madison
1972 [Iota Beta] Trenton, NJ City-Wide
1972 [Iota Gamma] New Mexico State
1972 [Iota Delta] Henderson State
1972 [Iota Epsilon] Eureka
1972 [Iota Zeta] Illinois Wesleyan
1972 [Iota Eta] Texas Christian
1972 [Iota Theta] Louisiana State
1972 [Iota Iota] Catholic
1972 [Iota Kappa] Arizona State
1972 [Iota Lambda] Uni. of Alabama-Birmingham
1972 [Iota Mu] Northwestern State
1972 [Iota Nu] Mobile, AL City-Wide
1972 [Iota Xi] California State (PA)
1972 [Iota Omicron] Uni. of Central Oklahoma
1972 [Iota Pi] Miami (FL), City-Wide
1972 [Iota Rho] Uni. of North Carolina-Charlotte
1973 [Iota Sigma] Mercer
1973 [Iota Tau] Middle Tennessee State
1973 [Iota Upsilon] Austin Peay State

1973 [Iota Phi] Chicago W Suburban City-W
1973 [Iota Chi] University of South Carolina
1973 [Iota Psi] Southeastern Oklahoma
1973 [Iota Omega] Southwest Texas State

K

1921 [Kappa] University of California-Berkeley
1973 [Kappa Alpha] University of Oklahoma
1973 [Kappa Beta] Jacksonville State
1973 [Kappa Gamma] Lander
1973 [Kappa Delta] West Georgia
1973 [Kappa Epsilon] Florida State
1973 [Kappa Zeta] Millikin
1973 [Kappa Eta] Milwaukee, WI City-Wide
1973 [Kappa Theta] Wisconsin Oshkosh
1973 [Kappa Iota] University of South Florida
1973 [Kappa Kappa] Baldwin-Wallace
1973 [Kappa Lambda] Syracuse
1973 [Kappa Mu] Sam Houston State
1973 [Kappa Nu] University of Evansville
1973 [Kappa Xi] Arkansas State
1973 [Kappa Omicron] U of NC-Chapel Hill
1973 [Kappa Pi] Delta State
1973 [Kappa Rho] University of Virginia
1973 [Kappa Sigma] East Carolina
1973 [Kappa Tau] Texas A & I
1974 [Kappa Upsilon] Auburn
1974 [Kappa Phi] University of Maryland
1974 [Kappa Chi] Louisiana Tech
1974 [Kappa Psi] Frostburg State

1974 [Kappa Omega] Uni. of CA - Santa Barbara

Λ   1947 [Lambda] University of Chicago
1974 [Lambda Alpha] Uni. of Wisc.-Whitewater
1974 [Lambda Beta] Clarion
1974 [Lambda Gamma] Millersville
1974 [Lambda Delta] Idaho State
1974 [Lambda Epsilon] Kansas City City-Wide
1974 [Lambda Zeta] University of Alabama
1974 [Lambda Eta] Old Dominion
1974 [Lambda Theta] Uni. of Arkansas-Fayetteville
1974 [Lambda Iota] Providence, RI City-Wide
1974 [Lambda Kappa] U of MD – Baltimore
1974 [Lambda Lambda] Ashland
1974 [Lambda Mu] Southern Arkansas
1974 [Lambda Nu] Paul Quinn
1974 [Lambda Xi] University of California - Davis
1974 [Lambda Omicron] Charleston (SC)
1974 [Lambda Pi] Grand Valley State
1974 [Lambda Rho] Northeast Louisiana
1974 [Lambda Sigma] University of Mississippi
1974 [Lambda Tau] Pacific CA
1974 [Lambda Upsilon] State College of Arkansas
1975 [Lambda Phi] Marquette
1975 [Lambda Chi] University of Texas-Arlington
1975 [Lambda Psi] University of Florida
1975 [Lambda Omega] Duke

M

1921 [Mu] University of Pittsburgh
1975 [Mu Alpha] VA Polytec. Instit. & State
1975 [Mu Beta] George WA, DC City-Wide
1975 [Mu Gamma] Ithaca
1975 [Mu Delta] Findlay
1975 [Mu Epsilon] University of Kentucky
1975 [Mu Zeta] U of Tennessee-Knoxville
1975 [Mu Eta] University of Arizona
1975 [Mu Theta] Lewis
1975 [Mu Iota] University of Central Florida
1975 [Mu Kappa] Uni. of Arkansas-Little Rock
1975 [Mu Lambda] New Mexico State
1975 [Mu Mu] Towson State
1975 [Mu Nu] Southern Mississippi
1975 [Mu Xi] Augusta State
1975 [Mu Omicron] North Carolina State
1975 [Mu Pi] University of Delaware
1975 [Mu Rho] Vanderbilt
1975 [Mu Sigma] Cameron
1976 [Mu Tau] University of New Orleans
1976 [Mu Upsilon] William and Mary
1976 [Mu Phi] Flint, MI City-Wide
1976 [Mu Chi] U of California - Riverside
1976 [Mu Psi] Baltimore, MD City-Wide
1976 [Mu Omega] Georgia Medical

N   1921 [Nu] Michigan
1976 [Nu Alpha] American
1976 [Nu Beta] Mississippi State
1976 [Nu Gamma] Northwest Missouri
1976 [Nu Delta] Southeastern Louisiana
1976 [Nu Epsilon] Minneapolis-St. Paul, City-Wide
1976 [Nu Zeta] Southeastern Massachusetts
1976 [Nu Eta] Gary, IN City-Wide
1976 [Nu Theta] Troy State
1976 [Nu Iota] Southern Methodist
1976 [Nu Kappa] West Florida
1976 [Nu Lambda] CA State. Uni. at Sacramento
1976 [Nu Mu] New Orleans(LA) City-Wide
1976 [Nu Nu]
1976 [Nu Xi]
1977 [Nu Omicron] University of Montevallo
1977 [Nu Pi]
1977 [Nu Rho] Maryland Eastern Shore City-Wide
[Nu Sigma]Charleston Southern
[Nu Tau] Georgia College & State
[Nu Upsilon] San Diego, CA City-Wide
[Nu Phi] Ohio Wesleyan
[Nu Chi] Utica College of Syracuse University
[Nu Psi] Radford
[Nu Omega]

Ξ 1922 [Xi] Louisville
1979 [Xi Alpha] Georgia Institute of Technology
1979 [Xi Beta] Winthrop
1979 [Xi Gamma]Long Island, NY City-Wide
1979 [Xi Delta]
1979 [Xi Epsilon]
1979 [Xi Zeta] Southeastern
1979 [Xi Eta] Georgia Southern
1979 [Xi Theta] Nicholas State University
[Xi Iota] Spartanburg, SC City-Wide
[Xi Kappa]
[Xi Lambda] California State-Fullerton
[Xi Mu]
[Xi Nu]Rutgers
[Xi Xi] California State Polytechnic-Pomona
[Xi Omicron]Francis Marion
[Xi Pi]Albany, NY City-Wide
[Xi Rho]
[Xi Sigma]
[Xi Tau] Cambrige, MA City-Wide
[Xi Upsilon]Birmingham -Southern College
[Xi Phi]
[Xi Chi]California State-Fresno
[Xi Psi] Pullman, WA Core
[Xi Omega]

O

1922 [Omicron] Nebraska
[Omicron Alpha] Queens, NY City-Wide
[Omicron Beta]
[Omicron Gamma]University of AL-Huntsville
1981 [Omicron Delta] Bennett College
1981 [Omicron Epsilon] MS Uni. for Women
1981 [Omicron Zeta] Oakland University
1981 [Omicron Eta] Uni. of NC - Greensboro
[Omicron Theta] Wittenberg
[Omicron Iota] Elon College
[Omicron Kappa] State Uni. of NY-New Paltz
[Omicron Lambda]
[Omicron Mu]
1982 [Omicron Nu]Uni. of NC at Pembroke
[Omicron Xi] Emory
[Omicron Omicron]LaSalle
1983 [Omicron Pi] SE Missouri State University
1983 [Omicron Rho]
1983 [Omicron Sigma]
1983 [Omicron Tau] Christopher Neport
1983 [Omicron Upsilon] West Virginia
1983 [Omicron Phi] Clemson University
1983 [Omicron Chi] Palo Alto/Santa Clara, CA
1984 [Omicron Psi] California State-Bakersfield
1984 [Omicron Omega] Texas A&M

Π

1923 [Pi] UCLA
1984 [Pi Alpha] New haven, CT City-Wide
[Pi Beta] Rochester, NY City-Wide
[Pi Gamma] Western Carolina
[Pi Delta]
[Pi Epsilon]
[Pi Zeta]
1985 [Pi Eta] State U of NY-Binghamton
1985 [Pi Theta] Dartmouth
[Pi Iota]
[Pi Kappa] Denison
[Pi Lambda]Iona College
1987 [Pi Mu] Longwood College
[Pi Nu]Southern College of Technology
[Pi Xi]
[Pi Omicron]Wake Forest
[Pi Pi]
[Pi Rho]
[Pi Sigma]State University of NY-Old Westbury
[Pi Tau]
[Pi Upsilon]
[Pi Phi]
1989 [Pi Chi] CA State - Dominguez Hills
[Pi Psi] University of California-Santa Cruz
[Pi Omega]

P

1924 [Rho] Columbia University
1989 [Rho Alpha] West Chester University, PA
1989 [Rho Beta] Southwest Missouri State
1990 [Rho Gamma] Memphis, TN City-Wide
[Rho Delta] University of Tulsa
1991 [Rho Epsilon] Princeton, NJ City-Wide
[Rho Zeta] Poughkeepsie, NY City-Wide
[Rho Eta] Baylor
[Rho Theta]
[Rho Iota] Harrisburg, PA Core
[Rho Kappa] Oberlin, OH City-Wide
[Rho Lambda] U of South Carolina-Aiken
[Rho Mu]Sag [Rho Nu]
[Rho Xi] Xavier(OH)
[Rho Omicron] Slippery Rock
1992 [Rho Pi] Edinboro, PA Core
[Rho Rho] University of Richmond
[Rho Sigma]
[Rho Tau]
[Rho Upsilon]
[Rho Phi]
[Rho Chi]
[Rho Psi]
[Rho Omega]

Σ

1924 [Sigma] Clark Atlanta Uni. (LA Alumnae)
[Sigma Alpha] University of North Florida
[Sigma Beta]
[Sigma Gamma]
[Sigma Delta] University of MO-Rolla
[Sigma Epsilon] Kennesaw State
[Sigma Zeta]
[Sigma Eta]
[Sigma Theta]
[Sigma Iota] Lynchburg College
[Sigma Kappa]
[Sigma Lambda]
[Sigma Mu]
1996 [Sigma Nu]
[Sigma Xi]
[Sigma Omicron] Utah State
[Sigma Pi]
[Sigma Rho] University of Alaska-Anchorage
[Sigma Sigma]
[Sigma Tau] California State-Stanislaus
[Sigma Upsilon]University of WI-Parkside
[Sigma Phi] University of Arkansas at Moticello
1997 [Sigma Chi] W. VA Wesleyan College
[Sigma Psi] U of the Virgin Islands-St. Thomas
[Sigma Omega]

T
  1924 [Tau] Wayne State
  1998 [Tau Alpha] Armstrong Atlantic State U
  1998 [Tau Beta] Indiana U of Pennsylvania
  1999 [Tau Gamma]Indiana-Fort Wayne City-Wide

Υ 1924 [Upsilon] USC

Φ 1925 [Phi] Drake

X 1925 [Chi] Indianapolis

Ψ 1925 [Psi] University of Kansas

Ω 1925 [Omega] Cleveland

Those are not all of the chapters of Delta Sigma Theta Sorority but it should give you an idea of how the organization has grown incredibly and multiplied itself throughout the years.

ABOVE

AND

BEYOND

AN UNAUTHORIZED HISTORY
OF DELTA SIGMA THETA

FIND HIDDEN MESSAGE

```
D E L I Z A P S H I P P E N E
O L I V E C J O N E S L T A S
D O O H R E T S I S A L P H A
E D U T I T R O F H O W A R D
D E L T A S I G M A T H E T A
M A M I E R E D D Y R O S E I
E D I T H M O T T E Y O U N G
N O I T A N I M R E T E D L G
N O I T A Z I N A G R O O M A
B E T A C H A P T E R V T H E
K C A L B F F U C L E H T E T
E T H E L C A R R W A T S O N
C R I M S O N A N D C R E A M
E T I H W N N E P E E R D A M
D N O Y E B D N A E V O B A A
```

FIND HIDDEN MESSAGE ON THE LEFT USING WORDS BELOW (ANSWER KEY ON PAGE 124):

ABOVEANDBEYOND
ALPHA
THE BETACHAPTER
CRIMSONANDCREAM
DETERMINATION
EDITHMOTTEYOUNG
ELIZAPSHIPPEN
ETHELCARRWATSON
ETHELCUFFBLACK
FORTITUDE
HOWARD
LOVE
MADREEPENNWHITE
MAMIEREDDYROSE
OLIVECJONES
ORGANIZATION
SISTERHOOD

for·ti·tude

Definition - strength of mind that allows one to endure pain or adversity with courage

CHAPTER FOUR
DELTA REGIMES AND DELTA TODAY

Delta Sigma Theta Sorority has grown dramatically. In 1919, they elected their first National President.

In this chapter the national presidents will be highlighted along with the years of their administration.

Sadie T. M. Alexander 1919-1923

Dorothy Pelham Beckley 1923-1926

Ethel LaMay Calimese 1926-1929

Anna Johnson Julian 1929-1931

Gladys Byram Shepperd 1931-1933

Jeannette Triplett Jones 1933-1935

Vivian Osborne Marsh 1935-1939

Elsie Austin 1939-1944

Mae Wright Downs 1944-1947

Dorothy I. Height 1947-1956

Dorothy P.. Harrison 1956-1958

Geraldine P. Woods 1963-1967

Frankie M. Freeman 1967-1971

Lillian P. Benbow 1971-1975

Thelma P. Daley 1975-1979

Mona H. Bailey 1979-1983

Hortense G. Canady 1983-1988

Yvonne Kennedy 1988-1992

Bertha M. Roddey 1992-1996

Marcia L. Fudge 1996-2000

Gwendolyn E. Boyd (2000 – present)

DELTA TODAY

National President:
Gwendolyn E. Boyd (2000 – present)

There have been twenty-two national Presidents of Delta Sigma Theta. If you notice all served for 2, 3, or 4 years with the exception of Dorothy I. Height that served 9 years respectively.

The current President oversees the Sorority's very important five-point program. Since Delta Sigma Theta's inception the sorority has made it very well known that they are an organization that strives to serve the African American community having a positive effect on America as a whole. The five point program consist of:

Physical and Mental Health

Educational Development

Economic Development

International Awareness and Involvement

Political Awareness and Involvement

Delta Today In the News (select headlines)

(Be sure to read some of the articles in order to get full details of what Delta is doing today. Titles, dates and publications are listed for you.)

Title: Sorority leader targets AIDS ' denial' among blacks
Date: 03-08-2002
Publication: The Washington Times

Staff writer Denise Barnes interviewed Gwendolyn E. Boyd, the 22nd national president of Delta Sigma Theta Sorority Inc. Question: The Deltas have a long history of community service. What are some of the projects the sorority is currently working on? Answer: [Tomorrow] Delta Sigma Theta Sorority Inc. will host an International Day of Service to address HIV/AIDS in the African American community.

Title: UC-Davis sorority highlights ethnic diversity through dance
Date: 12-07-2000
Publication: University Wire
Author: S.F. Zook

(The California Aggie) (U-WIRE) DAVIS, Calif. -- The University of California-Davis chapter of Delta Sigma Theta hosted its annual Multicultural Extravaganza show, featuring three new presentations from a variety of student organizations, Tuesday night. Gospel singer Tiffany Mouton, Na Keiki' O Hawaii and Phi Beta Sigma appeared at the extravaganza for the first time.

Title: After 24 years, store still helping clothe needy
Date: 03-28-2000
Publication: The Dallas Morning News
Author: Sharon Egiebor / Staff Writer of The Dallas Morning News

The Ruth K. Hickman Clothing Store is in a new location but with the same mission: offering free clothing to people in need. The store has moved to the Dr. Billy E. Dade Learning Center from the Sequoyah Educational Center. The store is a community service project of the Dallas Alumnae Chapter of Delta Sigma Theta Inc.

Title: U. Virginia sorority, community service group sponsor charity drive to benefit local foster children
Date: 12-03-1999
Publication: University Wire
Author: Adam Justice

(Cavalier Daily) (U-WIRE) CHARLOTTESVILLE, Va. -- Some University of Virginia students are helping to create their own "Toy Story" this holiday season. Collection boxes were scattered around Grounds for the past two weeks to collect toys for disadvantaged children. Sponsored by the University Guide Service and Delta Sigma Theta sorority.

Title: Delta Sigma Theta makes powerful return to Duke U.
Date: 04-21-1999
Publication: University Wire
Author: Anya Sostek

(The Chronicle) (U-WIRE) DURHAM, N.C. -- After a 3-year absence, the historically black sorority will induct 25 new members this spring After remaining inactive for three years, historically-black sorority Delta Sigma Theta will induct new members this spring.

Title: L.A. Deltas Join in Census 2000
Date: 03-17-1999
Publication: Los Angeles Sentinel

L.A. Deltas Join in Census 2000 The Los Angeles chapter of Delta Sigma Theta Sorority has joined the U.S. Census Bureau in its effort to get minorities counted in the 2000 census, officials recently announced. The sorority, one of the largest black organizations in the nation, has agreed to recruit census takers, who will help guarantee that African Americans and other minorities...

Title: Delta' s 86th Founders Day Features Renowned Author Iyanla Vanzant
Date: 02-16-1999
Publication: Michigan Chronicle

DELTA' S 86TH FOUNDERS DAY FEATURES RENOWNED AUTHOR IYANLA VANZANT A record-breaking audience of guests and members of the Detroit Alumnae Chapter of Delta Sigma Theta Sorority Inc. gathered on Saturday, Jan 16, to hear dynamic, best-selling author lyanla Vanzant. The 86th Founders Day theme was "At the Threshold of the 21st Century: Facing Forward, Looking Back."

Title: Indiana U.' s Delta Sigma Theta honors black culture
Date: 01-28-1999
Publication: University Wire
Author: Rachel Kipp

(Indiana Daily Student) (U-WIRE) BLOOMINGTON, Ind. -- In Lewis Carroll' s book "Alice in Wonderland," the characters held a pageant, called a Jabberwock, to celebrate the talent in their community. This week the members of the Delta Sigma Theta sorority are celebrating their own Jabberwock, honoring African and African-American culture while raising money for HIV/AIDS.

Title: Mikki Howard Headlines Delta Sigma Theta' s WOW Explosion
Date: 12-03-1998
Publication: Los Angeles Sentinel

Mikki Howard Headlines Delta Sigma Theta' s WOW Explosion The Inglewood Alumnae Chapter of Delta Sigma Theta Sorority Inc. is proud to announce that songtress Mikki Howard will headline its annual Arts and Letters Showcase entitled "The Wow Explosion: Exhibiting Women of Worth in the Arts" which is slated for Saturday, Feb. 27 1999 at 6:30 p.m.

**Title: Delta Sigma Theta Sorority Convenes
Largest Assembly in New Orleans**
Date: 10-13-1998
Publication: Columbus Times

Delta Sigma Theta Sorority Convenes Largest
Assembly in New Orleans, LA--Over 12,000
participants gathered in New Orleans for the 44th
National Convention of Delta Sigma Theta
Sorority, making it the largest biennial meeting
in the organization' s 85-year history.

**Title: SORORITY HELPS OUT WITH
BLACK HISTORY PROJECT**
Date: 02-10-1998
Publication: St. Louis Post-Dispatch

The late philosopher and activist W.E.B. DuBois
long ago wrote of educated African-Americans'
obligations to the less fortunate. Black
fraternities and sororities have tried to live up to
his ideal. Last week, local members of Delta
Sigma Theta Sorority Inc. helped sponsor a black

history program for St. Louis public school
students at Harris- Stowe State College.

**Title: BANK GIVES $50,000 TOWARD DAY
CARE CENTER**
Date: 10-18-1997
Publication: St. Louis Post-Dispatch
Author: Richard Collings

Plans to build a day care center in East St. Louis
got a boost Friday when NationsBank announced
it would donate $50,000 toward the project. The
Delta Sigma Theta Economic Development
Corp. is planning the center. "Our organization is
very excited," said Germaine Pang, president of
Delta Sigma Theta.

Title: SPEAKING OF EDUCATION:
Scholarship, Sisterhood, Service
Date: 06-12-1997
Publication: Black Issues In Higher Education

SPEAKING OF EDUCATION: Scholarship,
Sisterhood, Service When twenty-two young
Black women came together at Howard
University to form Delta Sigma Theta sorority,

their goal was to focus on scholarship, sisterhood, and service to the African American community. A review of the sorority' s early history indicates that these young women, and the ones who followed them, did exactly that.

Title: Mrs. Virgie Lean Butler, cited as Delta Sigma Theta' s 1997 Woman of
Date: 02-18-1997
Publication: Tennessee TRIBUNE, The
Author: None

Mrs. Virgie Lean Butler, cited as Delta Sigma Theta' s 1997 Woman of the. Year. Mrs. Virgie Lean Butler of Huntingdon, Tennessee, was recently honored as The Jackson Tennessee Alumnae Chapter of Delta Sigma Theta' s 1997 Woman of the Year. Mrs. Butler was cited for her involvement in church, community and civic work. She is a member of St. Paul Baptist Church, Huntingdon, Tennessee.

Title: Deltas lead fight for Alexis Herman
Date: 12-21-1996
Publication: Washington Afro-American
Author: James Wright

Deltas lead fight for Alexis Herman. Delta Sigma Theta (DST), the world' s largest Greek-letter sorority for Black women, is spearheading efforts to form a broad support network for the nomination of Alexis Herman as secretary of the U.S. Department of Labor. Ms. Herman is a member of the sorority and is presently the Special Assistant to the President for Public Liaison.

Title: Deltas honor 35 year member, NMA president
Date: 10-28-1995
Publication: New York Amsterdam News
Author: Elinor Tatum

Deltas honor 35 year member, NMA president. The members of the Queens Alumnae Chapter of Delta Sigma Theta Sorority Inc. hosted a gala reception to recognize chapter member Dr. Yvonnecris Smith Veal, newly installed president of the National Medical Association

(NMA), at the Robert Ross Johnson Family Life Center in St. Albans, Queens.

Title: Local Sorority Dedicates First Habitat Home
Date: 08-29-1995
Publication: Columbus Times
Author: Carol Gertjegerdes

Local Sorority Dedicates First Habitat Home. On Saturday, August 19 it seemed all roads lead to a single address on 30th Avenue. The temperatures soared, yet the heat did little to deter the more than 200 people who came out to witness history in the making. Members of the Columbus Alumnae Chapter of Delta Sigma Theta Sorority, Inc. were joined by politicians (local, state and national).

Title: BLACK SORORITY RAISED $1 MILLION IN 1994
Date: 07-17-1994
Publication: St. Louis Post-Dispatch
Author: None

Like most of the 185,000 members of Delta Sigma Theta, Bertha M. Roddey is a teacher. What the country' s largest black sorority continues to teach after 81 years, she says, is public service through education and economic development. More than 7,000 members from 44 states and overseas are renewing that commitment at the group' s 42nd national convention.

Title: Deltas reach out to youth
Date: 11-19-1994
Publication: Michigan Citizen
Author: Lisa K. Jennings

Deltas reach out to youth. Guns in the school, gangs, and more security were a few topics discussed at the "Kickin at the Town Hall Meeting". It was sponsored by Delta Sigma Theta Sorority Inc., Detroit Alumnae Chapter. Assistant Prosecuting Attorney Kym Worthy,

Deputy Police Chief Benny Napoleon, Judge Cynthia Stephens, and Director of Clean and Safe Schools.

Title: BUILDERS ON A BLITZ
Date: 07-24-1994
Publication: St. Louis Post-Dispatch
Author: Joan Dames

THE BIG BLITZ BUILD of Delta Sigma Theta sorority and Habitat for Humanity teamed professional skilled workers with hundreds of volunteers and left the metropolitan St. Louis area with 15 new homes for low- income families, seven in St. Louis and eight in East St. Louis. The Blitz Build drew volunteer workers of all races and creeds from across the community.

**Title: SORORITY REAFFIRMS ITS
MISSION MEETING HERE STRESSES
COMMITMENT**
Date: 07-20-1994
Publication: St. Louis Post-Dispatch
Author: None

If you' ve been anywhere near downtown this
week, you' ve seen them: thousands of black
women dressed in red and white. All are
members of Delta Sigma Theta sorority. About
7,000 of them have been in St. Louis this week
sharing ideas, stories, memories and hopes. But
more than anything, they are rededicating
themselves to their cause: helping the needy.

Title: Southfield Deltas present scholarships
Date: 06-14-1994
Publication: Michigan Chronicle
Author: Reginald Larrie

Southfield Deltas present scholarships. Delta
Sigma Theta Sorority Inc., Southfield Alumnae
chapter, began its celebration of May Week on
May 15 by worshiping at Hartford Memorial
Baptist Church. Peggy J. Harrell, Chapter
president, presented $1, 250 to Hartford' s
scholarship fund.

Title: WOMEN HOPE TO BUILD 15 HOMES IN A WEEK
Date: 05-09-1993
Publication: St. Louis Post-Dispatch
Author: Joan Foster Dames

With hammers and nails, two women are leading an effort to build 15 homes here for the needy, all in one week next summer. The women are: Gloria White, vice chancellor for human resources at Washington University and president of the St. Louis Alumnae Chapter member of Delta Sigma Theta sorority.

Delta Today is still the Delta of Yesterday. Holding own to their founders' vision of social activism and service to the community, you can easily see from the select news topics above the strong commitment from the members of Delta Sigma Theta Sorority Inc.

TEST YOUR DELTA IQ

PART TWO

Think you know much about Delta Sigma Theta? Well, since you were reading so closely, you should do fine on this quiz. And that doesn't mean you should peak back to the chapter for the answers – see what you can remember on your own! When you're done with the quiz, be sure to turn to the back of the book and write in your score.

Good Luck!

1) Which National President has served the longest term?
   a. Sadie T. M. Alexander
   b. Bertha M. Roddey
   c. Dorothy I. Height
   d. Frankie M. Freeman

2) In what year was Delta Sigma Theta founded at the University of Pennsylvania, the first Ivy League chapter?
   a. 1981
   b. 1918
   c. 1924
   d. 1938

3) Where is the Theta Nu Chapter of Delta Sigma Theta located?
   a. Oklahoma State University
   b. Harvard University
   c. Stanford University
   d. Texas A & M University - Commerce

4) Delta Sigma Theta is considered a...
   a. club for black men and wen
   b. for profit business association of black women
   c. national service organization
   d. network of black women that all believe the same

FAMOUS DELTAS

AND

PERSONALITIES

Barbara Jordan
(1936 – 1996)

Elected to the U.S. House of Representatives from Texas in 1972, Barbara Jordan became the first African-American congresswoman to be elected, and re-elected, from the Deep South. Before her election to Congress, she was a Texas State Senator, the first African-American woman to serve there.

Jordan captured the attention of the nation during the 1974 Nixon impeachment hearings. As a member of the House Judiciary Hearings she served on the committee charged with hearing and evaluating the evidence bearing on the possible impeachment of then-President Nixon. It was on this committee that her incisive questioning and her impassioned defense of the Constitution made her a respected national figure.

In 1976, Barbara Jordan became the first woman and first African-American to give the keynote speech at the Democratic National Convention. In 1978 she announced that she would not seek re-election and returned to Texas as a full professor at the Lyndon B. Johnson School of Public Affairs at the University of Texas. She remained there, and became a counselor to Texas Governor Ann Richards.

Wilma Rudolf
(1940 – 1994)

The first American woman ever to win three gold medals in the Olympics, Wilma Rudolph overcame major obstacles to make her mark in the record books and in life.

Rudolph contracted severe polio as a child. By age 16, she was an All-State basketball player and a bronze medalist in the 1956 Olympics. She attended Tennessee State University on a track scholarship, and returned for the 1960 Olympics - and Olympic glory, winning gold medals in the 100-meter dash, 200-meter dash and the 4 x 100-meter relay. She set world records in all three events. She was named United Press Athlete of the Year (1960), the AP Woman Athlete of the Year (1960, 1961) and received the Sullivan Award as the nation' s top amateur athlete (1961). She has been inducted into the Women' s Sports Hall of Fame and named one of five sports stars selected as America' s Greatest Women Athletes by the Women' s Sports Foundation, she is in the Black Sports Hall of Fame and the U.S. Olympic Hall of Fame. Rudolph gave women' s track a strong boost in America. Since her competition days, she has written a best-selling autobiography, Wilma, and created the Wilma Rudolph Foundation to train young athletes.

Mary McLeod Bethune
(1875 – 1955)

Mary Jane McLeod was born in South Carolina, the fifteenth of seventeen children. Scholarships enabled her to attend Scotia Seminary and Moody Bible Institute. Turned down when she applied to go to Africa as a missionary, she returned to the South. She met and married Albertus Bethune, and began to teach school.

In Daytona, Florida, in 1904 she scraped together $1.50 to begin a school with just five pupils. She called it the Daytona Literary and Industrial School for Training Negro Girls. A gifted teacher and leader, Mrs. Bethune ran her school with a combination of unshakable faith and remarkable organizational skills. She was a brilliant speaker and an astute fundraiser. She expanded the school to a high school, then a junior college, and finally it became Bethune-Cookman College.

Continuing to direct the school, she turned her attention to the national scene, where she became a forceful and inspiring representative of her people. First through the National Council of Negro Women, then within Franklin Roosevelt's New Deal in the National Youth Administration, she worked to attack discrimination and increase opportunities for Blacks. Behind the scenes as a member of the "Black cabinet," and in hundreds of public appearances, she strove to improve the status of her people.

Dorothy Height
(1912 -)

Delta Sigma Theta's tenth national longest serving
President. It is said of Dorothy Height that her lifetime
of achievement measures the liberation of Black
America, the advance of women' s rights and a
determined effort to lift the poor and the powerless.
Height began her career as a staff member of the YWCA
in New York City, becoming director of the Center for
Racial Justice. She became a volunteer with the National
Council of Negro Women, when she worked with
NCNW founder Mary McLeod Bethune. When Bethune
died, Height became president, a position she continues
to hold. NCNW, an organization of national
organizations and community sections with outreach to
four million women, develops model national and
international community-based programs, sent scores of
women to help in the Freedom Schools of the civil rights
movement, and spearheaded voter registration drives.

Height' s collaborative leadership style brings together
people of different cultures for mutual benefit. Since
1986, her belief in the importance of strong families has
been the primary energy behind the Black Family
Reunion Celebration in which almost 10 million have
participated.

Carol Moseley-Braun

Braun made history by being the first Black woman to be elected to the U.S. Senate in 1992. She currently serves as senator for the state of Illinois.

Johnetta B. Cole

Past President of Spelman College, Cole served her students well over the years and was embraced as "Sister President" by the Spelman students. In 1992, she was asked by President Clinton to help set the nation' s educational agenda.

Aretha Franklin

Franklin has rocked America for the past three decades and has generated 17 number-one songs. No wonder she is known as "The Queen of Soul".

Nikki Giovanni

Giovanni has made her mark in society as an innovative poet. Her latest book is entitled Racism 101. One of her poems that is an inspiration to all Black Women is "Ego Tripping".

Lena Horne

In addition to her dynamic voice as a singer, Horne has been greatly admired for her youthful beauty. At 80 years of age, she has performed all over the country for more than 60 years.

Betty Shabazz

Before her untimely death in 1997, Dr. Betty Shabazz was the Director of Communications and Public Relations for Medger Evers College of the City University of New York. She was also widely recognized as the widow of Malcolm X.

Niara Sudarkasa

Sudarkasa made history by becoming the first woman president of Lincoln University, America' s oldest historically Black College. Prior to he appointment at Lincoln, she made history by becoming the first Black woman to receive tenure at the University of Michigan.

Camille Cosby

Cosby has been extremely successful in her own rite. A philanthropist, Mrs. Cosby is an outspoken supporter of Historically Black Colleges and Universities. She is the wife of the famous actor Bill Cosby.

Judith Jamison

Jamison has astounded audiences for years with her graceful dancing style. She has danced with the Alvin Ailey dance troupe and has also organized her own modern-dance troupe - the Jamison Project. She currently works as the artistic director for the Alvin Ailey company.

Leontyne Price

This acclaimed opera diva has charmed audiences for several decades. Price has helped to open doors into this profession by becoming one of the first Black opera divas.

Ruby Dee

Dee is a famed Broadway and movie actress. Her credits include: "A Raisin in the Sun", "Taming the Shrew", "I Know Why the Caged Bird Sings", and "Do Tha Right Thang".

Nancy Wilson

Wilson has had over 30 albums on Billboard Charts and has produced a slew of hit records. She is a ballad singer with hits such as "Save Your Love for Me". Wilson also had an Emmy Award-winning series entitled "The Nancy Wilson Show".

...and so many more!

ABOVE

AND

BEYOND

AN UNAUTHORIZED HISTORY
OF DELTA SIGMA THETA

Answers to frequently asked questions about how to become a Delta are below, the answers are believed to be true but they are not infallible.

Question: How do I apply for membership for Delta Sigma Theta?

Answer: You will need to be an undergraduate student at a college seeking a degree or you can become a member through a graduate chapter if you already have a Bachelors Degree.

Question: What are the requirements and how do I go about applying?

Answer: If you are an undergraduate student, you must wait until the sorority have an announcement that they will be intaking new members, the announcement is sometimes called a "rush party" or interest meeting.

For graduate chapters, you will need to wait for a public announcement or a special invite to join.

All requirements will be given at the time of the interest meeting. Currently, the GPA requirement is 2.5.

Question: Can I apply through the national headquarters?

Answer: Generally, you must apply at a school you are attending while pursuing your undergraduate studies or via a graduate chapter.

Question: How much does it cost?

Answer: Fees and other cost will be given at the interest meeting.

Question: How does the selection process work?

Answer: If you have the requirements (GPA, letter of recommendation from a financially active Delta, public service) then the chapter members where you are applying for membership will vote on your acceptance and you will have to get the majority of the votes.

Question: What if I don't get the majority of votes?
Answer: You will not be accepted, but you will have the opportunity to try again so don't be negative!

Question: What will I have to do or go through if I do get accepted?
Answer: You are entering shaky ground, because this question refers to the process of what happens after you have been accepted.

So there is no better time than now to express the concerns and views of Nationals. Delta Sigma Theta Sorority Inc. prohibits any activities of hazing, pre-pledging or the likes thereof.

But the truth and reality of the matter is that chances are pretty high that some type of hazing activity will take place. In the case of applying for membership at an undergraduate chapter, you will have to be extremely careful when it comes to being pre-pledged or underground pledged. This is due to the young immature (not fully developed) minds that run the undergraduate organizations.

One would like to think that all of the young members of Delta Sigma Theta are

Scholars and extraordinary individuals like the Founders. But as with any organization or society, you will have bad seeds and these seeds are more prevalent on the undergraduate level so you will need to be cognizant of what actually goes on. Evidence, more than 20 chapters are currently on probation or serving a suspension for disciplinary reasons. And one can only imagine how many more chapters have issues of concern that has gone unreported.

It should be noted that the National Headquarters of Delta Sigma Theta Inc take swift and immediate action against any party that is found guilty of hazing, members are suspended and/or put on probation, while nonmembers can be banned from joining the sorority. Not to mention, that in most states hazing is a criminal offense.

The Catch 22. If you want to pledge Delta at an undergraduate chapter and the members found out and began taking advantage of you slightly, then you are put in an awkward position. If you say something they will not vote for you and if you do nothing you are accepting the rituals of hazing no matter how insignificant the hazing; it is still hazing. Then if you do get accepted, the members know that you are "cool" and the acts of underground pledging and hazing are taken to another level!

For an in depth discussion on hazing, underground pledging, the Do's and Don'ts while you are trying to get accepted to pledge then you must read *Pledge Brothers* (www.PledgeBrothers.com). The rules in *Pledge Brothers* are general but are extremely helpful when it comes to learning what to do and say and what not to do or say, as well as identify hazing and underground pledging in its rudimentary stages.

ΔΣΘ
DELTA SIGMA THETA

CHAPTER SIX
CONCLUSION

In conclusion, Delta Sigma Theta is an extraordinary organization founded by exemplary young ambitious and venturous women.

The organization has endured, multiplied and prospered since its 1913 founding.

Delta Sigma Theta's commitment to service has made it one of the few premier organizations in America.

God bless Delta Sigma Theta and its members so that they may continue to strive, achieve and service and let this book be a celebration of the rich history and legacy of a first class American Institution.

TEST YOUR
DELTA IQ
ANSWER KEY

PART ONE

1) C
2) A
3) B
4) B
5) B

PART TWO

1) C
2) B
3) D
4) C

HIDDEN MESSAGE PUZZLE
ANSWER KEY

```
D E L I Z A P S H I P P E N E
O L I V E C J O N E S L T A S
D O O H R E T S I S A L P H A
E D U T I T R O F H O W A R D
D E L T A S I G M A T H E T A
M A M I E R E D D Y R O S E I
E D I T H M O T T E Y O U N G
N O I T A N I M R E T E D L G
N O I T A Z I N A G R O O M A
B E T A C H A P T E R V T H E
K C A L B F F U C L E H T E T
E T H E L C A R R W A T S O N
C R I M S O N A N D C R E A M
E T I H W N N E P E E R D A M
D N O Y E B D N A E V O B A A
```

HIDDEN WORDS

ABOVEANDBEYOND
ALPHA
THE BETACHAPTER
LOVE
DETERMINATION
EDITHMOTTEYOUNG
ELIZAPSHIPPEN
FORTITUDE
HOWARD

MADREEPENNWHITE
MAMIEREDDYROSE
OLIVECJONES
CRIMSONANDCREAM
ORGANIZATION
SISTERHOOD
ETHELCARRWATSON
ETHELCUFFBLACK

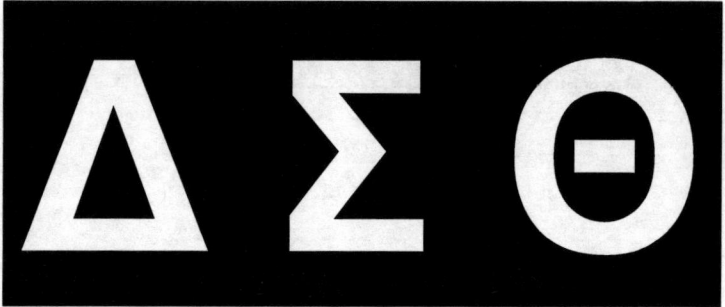

Δ Σ Θ

DELTA SIGMA THETA

ABOUT THE AUTHOR

Walter "Big Walt" Anderson, a Texas native, is an author, filmmaker and entrepreneur. Disciplined in the intricate field of Chemistry, he received his degree from Texas A & M University – Commerce.

If you wish to contact the author, go to:

BIGWALT.COM

God-Made, God-Sustained